Without Wheels

Sterling Warner

In the Grove Press
Fresno, California
2005

Without Wheels

Without Wheels. Copyright © 2005 Sterling Warner
In the Grove Press
Poetry Series Editor, Lee Herrick
PO Box 16195
Fresno, CA 93755
www.inthegrove.net

This book may not be reproduced in whole or part, in any form (beyond that permitted by Sections 107 and 108 of the U. S. Copyright Law and by reviewers for the purpose of criticism and review), without written permission of the publisher.

Printed in the United States of America.
Typeset by Mike Cole.
First Printing 2005.
Second Printing 2014.
ISBN-0-9740448-3-0

Acknowledgements

Most of the poems in *Without Wheels* appeared in one form or another in the *Leaf by Leaf* Literary Magazine over the past 12 years. Additionally "Listening to Nakai" appeared in *inside english* while "Image" and "Earth 'n Shadow" were published in *In the Grove*.

Table of Contents

Sterling Warner
Without Wheels

Nature's Corsage 1
    Timpani 2
    Listening to Nakai 3
    Jessica 4
    Earthquake Carole 5
    Lift the Skirt off Morning's Face (Golden Gate Park) 6
    San Diego Zoo 7
    Bougainvilleas 9

Around Corners 11
    Bag Lady: Queen of the Heavens 12
    Third Street 13
    Sea Breeze 14
    Along the Way 15
    Greyhound 16
    Black Leather 17
    Washington D.C. 18
    Keyboarding 19
    driftin' memories 20

The Critic 21
    Internet Concubines 22
    Gambling Boats and Bus Trips 23
    A Time No Clocks Signal 25

Compassionate Suburbanites	26
Unintentional Recruitments	28
Appeals	29
Note	30
We Used to Write Letters	31
Curtain Calls, Las Vegas	32

All the Way Home 33

Image	34
To My Nurse: Recollections of a 14 Year-old Boy with a Fractured Skull and Foxy RN	35
Messin' With the Magi	36
The Lab	38
Dragonfly	39
Aftermath	40
Tomales Bay	42
Without Wheels	43

Over the Shoulder 45

Directions	46
Tracy and Ricardo	48
Courtship on TWA	50
Birdlegs	51
Sylvia and I	52
Earth 'n Shadow	53
The Entertainer	55
The Actress	57

I.
Nature's Corsage

Timpani

there is strength in skin
stretched tautly across the body
        of another
two drumheads face to face
       flesh to flesh
       tightness giving way momentarily
to pressure: a tap, a touch, a kiss, a caress—
a celebration of tenderness lost in tension

there's beauty in a moment
when quarreling hearts and callused hands
both become soft and malleable;
a rarified power emerges
as personal vulnerability's disregarded
       focusing—
if only for a second—
on an eternity which will never be

Listening to Nakai

I.

Wooden throated flute song
winds no horse trainer can harness
travel back and forth soothingly, lightly, like
downy feathers floating
breeze back in spring, settling
nowhere, just filling a void
rising, fading, reappearing on horizon's forehead
slapping watercolor granite mountains, bouncing
back into the valley invigorated,
reinvented, falling into Dawn's cupped
hands, liberated from nightfall's silent embrace.

II.

Nakai, I hear you, like
whispering reeds, notes bunch together
only to push apart. Bear
walks between us, claws bark from
imaginary trees—I shudder, the
cacophony sending me to smoky
dens, iniquity's stepchildren,
elders cross-linking
saplings and bone to fortify structures
shaping today's creations, a balancing
act framing future losses . . . still listening,
listening to fluttering birds on wing,
sunlight's noon advancement,
twilight's amorous fan,
starlight's flirtatious wink,
spontaneously accepting the
wavering wooden flute voice
nakedly shaking like a nervous lover,
clothes falling to the floor apprehensively, yet
in perfect accord with the moment.

Jessica

Part love child, part Goth, Jessica
Never removed her shades
Unless in bed, lights out
Preserving Aphrodite's face with touches of mysterious mist;
Turntable attitudes, electrified legs, amplified ecstasy
Struck all like Steinway keys, spines rolling Westward,
Eyes anchored on alleyways, ebon,
San Francisco's stop lights blinking,
Accentuating, adding depth to
Eternal darkness.

Jessica knew these nights, those streets
Where her xylophone enthusiasm spread
Like light rails curving,
Always moving somewhere:
A streetcar, a flick, a concert, a recycler, 'til
One pair of late evening's arms lifted J's
Energies indefinitely, indiscriminately, leaving
Only a fixed mouth, tightly grimacing above her
Limp body
Elegantly poured into a paisley pant suit.

I write this now, not that I loved
I will this to Jessica, not that I cared . . . still the
Honesty behind her convictions
Like a parasol enigma
Breathed life into Haight Ashbury's paralysis—
San Franciscan possibilities.

Earthquake Carole

Pavement, dirt, steel and stone pulled and buckled
    in agony, the earth shook all its man-made manacles
        the ornaments called progress from her ever changing face.

Bridges collapsed; stone structures fell
    the Marina blaze lit the sky
        fiercely feeding on natural gas.

Batteries powered radios and T.V. sets
    people gathered outside their homes
        waiting to resume a lifestyle of convenience.

Many had nothing to return to at all: rubble, ash, and debris
    others—by the second aftershock—were printing T-Shirts boasting:
        I Survived the '89 Quake, oblivious to all but opportunity.

Media reports on fatalities varied
    some claimed 250 died while others estimated 500
        with the wounded listed in the thousands.

Yes, the media had no less than a field day
    the Giant's got a second chance at the World Series
        and Carole's 40th birthday ushered in a Bay Area event.

Lift the Skirt off Morning's Face
(Golden Gate Park)

Lift the skirt off morning's face
Drop funnels of light into a singular purpose
Sunrays like red gills inhaling oxygen from rising fog

Across the way, park people dwell in a world of
Makeshift grass beds, awaking to sounds of pooper-scoopers,
The wealthy picking up after the only shit they admit spreading

Like stowaways hidden in darkly lit rooms
Evading luxury liner doves jumpstarting relationships,
Golden Gate homeless disappear into shrubbery as badges emerge

Tag the skies with "Surrender Dorothy;"
Recall the cradle of "be-ins" and sidewalk artisans
Chant with Krishnas, dance to memories of Santana playing the Panhandle,

As major league baseball players, cursing like sailors, picking their noses
Scratching their crotches, spitting tobacco juices receive
More dignity, and respect than transients—freethinking philosophers

Whatever happened to Eric Burdon? His
Outsider impression of Golden Gate days and San Franciscan Nights
Spoke to multitudes of young dreamers, vagabond *young Turks*

Pleat dusk's shadow; rib it with luminescence,
Liberate the Japanese Garden for Tea—and squirrels
Open walkways to the De Young Museum; Willie's back in town

San Diego Zoo

on a balmy April afternoon
the San Diego Zoo
had everything
Hollywood could want
for a formula picture:
the pathos of birth,
long horn onyx dropping its foal.
    eros in spring heat,
a giraffe awkwardly mounting another—
missing its target,
but pursuing with purpose
    catastrophe from above
as a skyfari seat
frees itself
falling
upon
the rain forest aviary.

all is not what is seems.
concrete offers a
limited habitat;
leopards mark off
ten feet and pace
back and forth, and
lions lay limply on the
crudely sculpted hills
staring indifferently at
visitors from
all parts of the world . . . .
meanwhile children make monkey sounds
to stir indolent apes
oblivious to the numerous signs
that read:

Please Do Not
annoy, torment,
pester, plague,
molest, worry,
badger, harry,
harass, heckle
persecute, irk,
bullyrag, vex,
disquiet, grate,
beset, bother
tease, nettle,
tantalize or
ruffle the animals

Bougainvilleas

From the heart of her station wagon
She pulled a potted bougainvillea
Set it at our doorstep
Left word she'd park downwind, the
Street where her children
Could relieve themselves in an
Orchard, or sleep between vinyl seats
Undisturbed by car lights, burglar systems, or
Midnight window taps,
Courtesy of the county sheriff.

And where was your husband, the gardener?
He who draped the car's side windows
Like an old Volkswagen van
Bringing privacy to your Michelin-held household.
Why spend the money on plants for us?
Your children seemed hungry, or so I heard,
Their clothes soiled,
Faces filthy, painted with the same patches, the
Psoriasis, nervous rash.

I recall how Santa Cruz residents
Emptied hot tubs at local heath clubs when
You entered.
(I never stared but had a fertile imagination)
They were cruel,
I was quiet (too quiet),
You were simply nature's canvas; and you
Alone passed her brushstrokes onto
Another generation—such progeny
(Sylvia Brown, renowned psychic and
Your special physician, never forecast that
While delivering oracles
About your child-mother, did she?)

Images of you in the front seat
Wiping a bloody face against your bosom
While others scratched windows,
Kissed the cool glass, licked the imprints of
Each other's lips, aping the antics of grown-ups
Face to face, mouth to mouth
Persisted for weeks, though
You, the car, the children vanished
Long before I heard you'd stopped by
Or could consider how I'd
Quarter your family—bougainvilleas all—
At least for a night
In my home office.

II.
Around Corners

Bag Lady: Queen of the Heavens

With dignity and grace
the bag lady lifts the metal lids of Dixie-dumpsters
deftly skirting through the trash like an archaeologist
discovering treasures—remnants of a lost world, in part,
discarded gateways—always shut—to living standards
she now considers artifacts, buried in youthful debris.

Abstract memories—recaptured, collected and arranged
like a Smithsonian exhibition—
become addressed individually with monologues
assuring her *past* a place in the *present*
before the former slips from her visage forever
without acknowledgement or recognition.

This woman who owns the streets, parks, and alleyways
clings tightly to her cotton home—
a bedroll she carries by her side: spring, summer, fall, and winter—
and she invites people to cross her most recent threshold
swept clean with a counter brush,
hanging like a medallion around her neck.

Wearing her closet as proudly as Inanna, Queen of the Heavens,
she absorbs the odors of smog, subways, factories, and the street
reminding everyone she's the city's child—its messenger, its product;
after blessing all children and potential benefactors, the bag lady's
cryptic phrases and gestures anoint pedestrians with her pain, yet
they offer her, in return, only stares and consternation.

Third Street

Ceiling mirror reflects
nude bodies
moving like kelp
amid waterbed tides, a
wooden telephone
cable spool coffee table,
bullet holes sprayed
across the walls
ventilate, releasing pressures
in the East Lake Stick Victorian
each day looking past words like
"My father'd kill you
if ever you'd hurt me."

But you were the wild one,
adventurer, provocateur
boyfriends at your doorstep
2:30 in the morning, me
never knowing to whom you
said, "Go away,"
the young acolyte
from the nearby Catholic church,
(you always said you liked 'em
young; I was no exception), or
the guy next door who
threw bowie knives at trees, who'd
eye me like an oak stump as I
approached your door.

Crab grass, scattered clumps,
grew outside your window
aping romantic progress within
apologies became inappropriate;
after cooling it for a while,
nothing remained to
rekindle the flame . . . that flicker
which set the Red, White, and Blue Beach ablaze
expired—fixed into the skies like
Cassiopeia, a place I couldn't follow.

Sea Breeze

Bunch, I remember, lived
    above the Sea Breeze Bar
A flaky, turquoise structure
    incongruous to its surroundings
With antiquated Venetian blinds
    always dusty, always askew.

Outside lurked transients and burn-outs
    day and night
Faces that carried the raw, placid look
    of uncooked perch filets
Feverishly attempting to sustain themselves
    on cheap liquor and scraps from trashcans.

Yeah, Sue Bunch once resided there
    above the Sea Breeze and its patrons
And while her hands became stiff, course, and hard
    clutching keys, apprehensive and defensive
The peppered chowder smiles of those below her
    never even knew she existed.

Along the Way

Salt marshes, shopping cart graveyard,
Voracious mudslides suffocating tilt pour houses.
Rolling steel wheels halt only long enough to view
Richmond plastics:
Splintered windows, ghostly shades,
Gutted, burnt out interior, still recognizable by
Stubborn Brick, charred and miserable but
Ever defiant against despair.

We all jumped off that train,
Slept in the decayed monastery,
Felt spiritual awakenings.
In the presence of
An ecological wasteland.
Salt marshes offered renewal.
Never to come back,
Never to wash hands in
Motionless, gray-green pools,
Water looking like the remains of flotsam jetsam;
We linked minds in a moment of satisfaction,
A minute of resolution, an eternity of hope.

The 21st century's a
Long way from Yasgur's farm;
I want to tell Joni,
There is no "garden" to which we may return—
No "stardust golden" among oil refineries in
Pittsburgh, California.

Greyhound

The Greyhound express to San Francisco
    smells like sulfur, onions and Lysol,
Its tacky floor sucking the soles
    of swiftly passing shoes.
The seats, they lean back, and though curiously moist
    you casually recline--try to read
While overhead lights flicker and
    dark soupy matter sloshes in your ashtray.

On to the highway
    the bus crawls and sneers
    at motorists who shun its chamber
    who prefer traveling with known company.
Forward the bus moves
    vibrating like a gigantic dildo
and as the highway caresses it, the bus responds
    like an earthworm above ground.

Diverse passengers, young and old
    some stink of Vicks; others reek of wine.
Carry-ons range from fine Gucci leather purses
    to handbags held together with duct tape.
No one bothers to pass judgment;
    no one converses!
No one even looks beyond two seats, and
    no one's upset if the silver dog sputters--or dies;
It's to be expected.

Black Leather

Black leather jacket shuts out the chill of Milwaukee,
brings on the comfort of summer, as
parcels of land pass under steel birds of the sky and
exchange songs of locusts with the roar of lion throated engines—
a harmony sounding like water bubbling through kazoo—
past bays of green and automated dairies and
hoards of cheese

Refill all glasses with rosin, not wine.
Let us step feather-like into dance and
mojo in Wisconsin, with the
hand-crafted patience and precision of a Harley, and
crackle in the twilight on lacquered hardwood floors,
each footstep creating an eternal cacophony

Onward Wisconsin, so the song goes.
How well I miscast clairvoyance in Madison—
predicting Jessica Lange's first and last film
after her debut in *KING KONG*—
Wisconsin, yeah, Wisconsin,
solitary or sparse trees and rock formations,
enthrall the populace like a lonely Hollywood hero, but
dice my appetite for such stature, fame and fortune, instead,
let Lady Forward guide my ambition—
immortalize me no more than Peter Fonda—
save me a little imagination.

Washington D.C.

Museums, monuments, memorials, and merchants
    vie for public attention
        three t-shirts for a dollar commemorates
everything in Washington D.C.
    from Japanese Cherry Trees to the Smithsonian Castle,
        Georgetown to Ford's theater,
            the capitol dome to the National Gallery of Art.

The weeping octogenarians
    pushed about in wheelchairs by daughters—or granddaughters,
        sons—or grandsons, people who smother
            the liver-spotted hands with kisses, and
point out the Hope Diamond's sheer radiance, then
    turn the wheelchairs toward a cavern like elevator,
        dropping into the antiquated gut of the Natural History Museum
            leaving sobs that echo and linger behind cold steel doors.

Keyboarding

With attitude,
cyberspace surfers hammer away,
tenaciously strike keyboards, like
Diamondhead matchsticks
flashing across flint faced boxes.

Seven on seven processions,
saintly virtues, deadly sins,
parade across the Internet like
medieval mystery and morality plays,
masques, inviting audience interaction
focal points expanding, as alluring
as exotic perfume drifting
indiscriminately in all directions....
hair sticking to shoulders like
damp mink, rich, thick;
ain't no real lovin' there,
only allergenic paramedics,
ghoulish Dr. Scholl's innuendoes
lace white, bridal gown fingertips
in touch with screen saving scrapbooks, as
surreal as a Dali lip bleed.

driftin' memories

Who'd a thought I'd outlive myself
sifting through memories of
Golden Gate Park &
recollections of Hendrix, Joplin,
Lennon, Cass, Morrison, Redding;
Monterey stage, '67, like an altar
Woodstock, a dream fabliaux
Altamont, a nightmare--an
unraveled tapestry of ideals
taken as far as they'd go then
tested under protection of
leather angels; the
"bottom had fallen out" and
with it our determinism.

Somewhere nearby,
Garcia's guitar licks crack
open the night as the
Elvis generation slips into hazy
Ed Sullivan nostalgia,
their children tripping, days on the green
the Filmore, Avalon Ballroom, Winterland,
thinking 'bout times and people
offers little more than a heartbeat,
a familiar rhythm, a comforting moment
before the soul's solitary percussion becomes a
frozen metronome, beating alone then not at all.

III.
The Critic

Internet Concubines

Baby-boomers rub wrinkle-cream across the landscape of their dreams
To recapture the idealism and commitment of another era, a different spirit
Caught up in the locomotion, the frenzy of
Facing forward, never reflecting on technology by,
Distancing modernization like the Amish or Victorians, or
Their youthful, untethered, principle extremes;
"Power to the people" becomes "muscle to middle management." Then
Internet concubines celebrate the software solstice and
Conceal mid-drift mysteries or underweight fetishes though the
Magic of their electronic romances—or "buddy list" quickies.
Yes, B. Dylan, those times keep changing and the people tag along for
Necessity and approval.
Gen Xers defy the sincerity of their parents and stake claims on
Web sites—street corners of a different sort—selling their souls
To upgrades, consolidators, research engines, email accounts, and
Promises of independent business opportunities in the nude

        Jesus is a liberal;
        Belinda is a player;
        Juan rides the lottery; and,
        Lam writes PC programs.
        Been through passive resistance
        Danced at the disco,
        Slammed during Raves, and
        Scratched with the DJs

Until every outrage becomes mainstream, and
We observe our uniqueness in conformity.

Gambling Boats and Bus Trips

Gambling boats and bus trips to Reno
Lift spirits of people
Going somewhere, anywhere to
Create new beginnings,
Gain legacies passed on to grandchildren.
Casino vitality
Suspends lost hopes,
Buries dead dreams
Distances unemployment lines,
Freeway off ramps, and K-Mart specials.
Roulette wheels pass no judgment; slot machines
Spin animated promise,
Paper-thin potential to
Cash in on elusive jackpots that
Hit often enough to keep pulses rapid,
Sure that the next one will
Herald their deliverance.

Gambling cars, silver bullets to Las Vegas pass
Graveyard flowers hanging off Styrofoam wreaths,
So full of life, so tied to death, they seek
Purification—optimistic renewal
Like self cleansing cat boxes,
Genesis recasts itself
Devoid of desultory patriarchy.
Still the buses, the boat trips, the train rides increase
More frequent, possibly satisfying,
Perfect for people
Leading "good lives"
Ideal for bodies in need of a dream, where
Loose ends knot with "next time" or
"If only."

Gambling boats and busses to all things Nevada,
last chance to catch Sigfried and Roy,
the dusty wagering Mecca becomes
veil black, wrapped in evening faces,
glittering neon as shade advances,
transforming winning numbers into
extreme adult amusement parks, where the
only ticket's one's last paycheck,
collateral, one's house,
qualifications, unbridled passion.

A Time No Clocks Signal

A time no clocks signal, when
men in turtleneck sweaters accentuate
pear-shaped bodies, &
women sport blue stockings,
more frequently to
mask varicose veins than
make fashion statements.

Ah, we're all so complex we
would be islands of mystery,
forever, if not for an evaporating fog,
lifting mists
cloaking intimacies, &
in our nakedness
we deal with guilt & shame
forgetting that beauty
includes change, that
change requires "letting go," & that
"letting go" initiates journeys where
the only retreat's in further advancement.

A time no clocks signal, when *still life*
drawing classes invite senior citizens to model,
faces being "interesting" rather than common:
lined, wrinkled, weathered—old . . .
when arms become tight, sore, & feeble &
legs demand a walker &
feet slip into chic orthopedic shoes.
Graveyards & crematoriums become
as familiar with the company of loved ones;
friends & family
now gather only at funerals,
reunions where fewer & fewer participate.

Compassionate Suburbanites

Compassionate suburbanites demand
bottled Bushmill's wisdom
dartboard veracity,
innocence as vulnerable as heads
enclosed in wafer-thin shower caps amid
Amazonian rainforests.
Ain't it grand hangin' onto each other,
decorating skin
with grommet certainty, watching Sistas
sell time-shares on psychic networks, while
young adults demonstrate commitment to fine arts,
elevating vagina and penis monologues
to the status of high theater?

Between bingeing and dieting,
suburbanites cover themselves in
alabaster creams and mineral rich plasters
like mastodon preservation projects,
eager for appreciation and study,
gentle touches, grave conjecture—
dreaming of mice and minions
between rush-hour work commutes,
embracing fleshy pleasures—
inseparable unions, relationships
resonating like sewing needle strums during
guitar string sex—exuding
exotic tea-bag warmth,
banal lives, like slipped disks
searching for vertebrae—crookbacked from the start—
overshadowed by the crime of the century
hooking with all the grandeur of
celebrity coat hangers,

angst arm in arm with uptown charity,
attitude and hope like coffee-colored
mist filling skies gone blue-grey,
glancing off identical tract home eaves,
suffocating churchyard statues,
huddling against government monuments,
clinging to dead-end suburb debris like
tobacco residue absorbed in
cotton sweater fibers.

Unintentional Recruitment

Nothing's like

that unsolicited best friend

who hovers and hounds you

while you brush each earful

aside,

divert another's proud mention of

US

immortalizing small talk with the

perseverance of Vaseline

rubbed into red damask furniture, or

pressed beneath bootheels and Niki's

always there, always noticeable,

always lonely, yet

seldom quiet or solitary

Appeals

Heard the cry of a harmonica
pulling left to right like rolling seizures,
seismographic invitations to social convulsions—
    paradigm shifts, reinvented wheels,
unable to turn, frozen to shorter legs that stretch across
life's wasted canyon, a pit hosting suburbs of
cockroaches—*real* clients, *unabashed consumers*,
still, there's never enough space for track homes, and golf courses, and
    shopping malls, and video arcades, and banks.

Saw veins of smoke pulsate above a mortuary
sailing spiritually into the stratosphere
testimony to itself and a town below,
    only place I know where management misspells *laughter;*
break it down man, break it down;
break the rhetoric down, & beat life's body politic
wafer thin, beyond oppression, trading
    cat's claw smirks for a chuckle—with reason—instead of
        daily exercises in damage control.

Note

I watched
t.v. the other night
a public broadcasting network
and in between ringing phones
for membership drives
I saw a special.
a man said
the sixties
were an excuse
for bad poetry
that arts never flourished again until
Ronald Reagan set the country back
thirty years:
socially, economically, industrially.

my neighbor laughed at so called *liberals*
said he was better *off now* than before
the eighties
then found himself out of his
short-term job—
long on promise—
a year latter.
he now sleeps at
the homeless shelter
eats at Martha's Soup Kitchen,
courtesy of the Catholic church
which he secretly
despises.

the man on PBS and
the beggar in the street seem
one and the same,
lacking authentic dignity
or humility
both seeking a willing mark
to exchange a tale of actual or impending misery
for a dollar.

We Used to Write Letters

We used to write letters
bucket cherries from virgin orchards
eat watermelon
overhanging dry creek beds in
stately oak arms
spitting seeds where
we imagined they'd sprout or be eaten.

Sitting on curbs, we'd watch
big rigs drive down main street,
roll rotten oranges between tires,
flip off drivers who wouldn't blast horns, and
dare them to move an inch closer—
god, we were dramatic.

We used to think never'd come a day our
legs weren't eager to march or protest . . .
when donations to the AFL/CIO,
Amnesty International, and Save the Whales
would supplant vigorous participation;
accosting the world with existential queries,
we expected timely answers—thought
authoritative figures accountable;
generation gaps became apparent, told
"This is America; love it or leave it,"
we—the future—disillusioned, dissatisfied,
disappointed champions of social activism, change.
persevering with a difference,
cherishing simple gestures, discreet movements,
veins flowing through grass blades.

Curtain Call, Las Vegas

And yes, I'm getting older when
Jethro Tull, Elvin Bishop, Tina Turner start
Doing the Elvis gig in Las Vegas
Former stomping grounds of Lawrence Welk
Hipsters, Peggy Lee's fever, Pat Boone's packaging and
Tony Bennett's banter.

Now Howard Stern replaces Don Rickles,
Jewel, Dr. Dre, Ricky Martin, Brittany Spears
Hang backstage, waiting to turn up easy street
Amid their waning adulation.
Kicking it, taking in the licks, the lyrics, the
Official vocabulary of each new lost generation, a
Plethora of defining keystones,
Generation gaps, and
Enshrined misunderstandings.

And yes, Bob Dylan's coming to town,
"Like a rolling stone," mercilessly grinding
Wayne Newton's ulcerous legacy—following
Decades of lacy underwear, affectionate tokens,
Sexual barrages.
Now geriatric curtain calls shower Mr. Las Vegas—
Faint sepia images of past glories
Flash through his mind like sharp, electric jolts
Brief, numbing and unfulfilling, passing beyond,
Disappearing into the crisis cesspool, identity morgue,
Superstar mausoleum.

IV.
All the Way Home

Image

Sometimes I'm aware that
I took the time to
glance
at my passing image
in a mirror,
something I'd never done
ten years ago—two years ago;
searching more for
a passing notion, a better face,
a more satisfying self-image.

My father would practice
smiling
after he shaved,
once his red hair and ivory teeth were brushed—
following the mint flavored ritual
of pulling and tugging waxed strings
lifelines with which he flossed.
Ah, father too, looked deep into his reflection
longing for the purity not guaranteed by one's
straight incisors.

No antique, beveled mirror
framed with coral, sea shells and
Elmer's glue
provide me a screen to dream on, to look in
and father needs no looking glass to remind him
of his passing.
Still, each time I move swiftly by
windows, mirrors, and polished metal
my mind's eye catches dad,
watching, waiting,
wondering when I'll acknowledge the smile
that is his—and begin to practice it perfectly.

To My Nurse:
Recollections of a 14-Year-Old Boy with Fractured Skull & a Foxy R.N.

You helped me with all my personals,
   lord knows I wouldn't have had it any different!
But you made my recovery needlessly tougher,
   all I asked for was a kiss—all I did was suffer.

I laughed as you cleaned me,
   slapping powder on my buttocks,
Your hands felt so soft, so sensuous, so nimble;
   (you even said once or twice I was cute)
Such apparent interest only compounded desire
   encouraged I continued my bed-ridden suit.

As you fed me I teased you—I did it to please you
   why didn't ya feel my pulse more often?
Was I just young and silly, crooning,
   "I love you—really,"
Sighing each day you'd walk in,
   "Nurse, have pity?"

Messin' With the Magi

Pain inspires the most reluctant Magi
to part with trash or lay out gifts;
my fractured skull invited many riches, many Magi
the brave white hunter, my taxidermist uncle,
gave me leather scraps and fur, which I
rapped about my feverish, aching body and
wore in thin strips over throbbing temporal lobes.

Generous friends provided entertainment, setting
boxes of old game boards at the foot of the bed
noticeably satisfied as they sacrificed
discolored cardboard containers—
spilt at four corners—
missing dice, instructions, game pieces
minute timers, and play money.

Old food—yes food, like blackened bananas
appeared on plastic platters,
bringing small life to my room.
Like Corinthian columns, dented soup cans,
piled straight and high,
cluttered corners once neat and my Magi
rewarded a hunger for comfort
with fruit and vegetables—
Betty Crocker, Duncan Hines, Nabisco and Pillsbury,
Laura Scudders, Quaker Oats, and *Paul Newman's Own* . . . .
Like a barrel on a transit bus during a food drive,
I became a depository, a vestibule,
for gracious cast-offs from cup-boards, and
dated items on stock shelves

An ax (or was it a drummer?) embedded in my head
unleashed my equilibrium, spread nauseous tides
through the highways of my veins,
provided me endless concerts of
viscously hammered tubular bells.

Abstinence in movement—no prodding, no smiling,
no acknowledgement of Magi in my presence—
translated into ingratitude to star following pilgrims,
kings and queens from as far away as Fresno.
My Magi walked away from my manger
dissatisfied, dejected, disappointed
my head did not lighten, loosen, or heal with their treasures of
isopropyl incense, frankincense and myrrh.

The Lab

Other fathers took their kids
   to playgrounds, parks, museums and zoos.
But my siblings and I would go to a laboratory
   to spin water in Dad's huge centrifuge.

We'd peer through microscopes—at our hair and spit
   then fight to autoclave blood agar plates;
Swabbing each other with alcohol, giving imaginary shots
   little doctors and grave scientists, among beakers and pipettes.

No, we never worried about common excursions
   our trips to convalescent homes were unique.
We were Dad's little assistants (though we tripped on our lab coats)
   and cared very little about what others would think.

Acetone, iodine, isopropyl, ether;
   we knew these chemicals; we cherished their smells.
To us they were Dad and with Dad we were safe
   to explore strange worlds of microbes and cells.

Dragonfly

High-top black tennis shoes trip
over dirt clods and brush in vacant lots . . .
move tirelessly back and forth—touching
every inch of the vast perimeter,
socks catching foxtails like Velcro,
chasing allusive dragonflies,
settling for less.

Arms viciously slash air
hands clutch nets—
old wire hangers and mom's newer nylons—
(we always *borrow* two)
catch little more than wind gusts and
undaunting determination

Brother Dave stalked front yard flowerbeds
I stood sentry in back, waiting for
expectant air to deliver insect trophies I'd
drop into empty mayonnaise jars
bedded with chloroform-doused cotton.

Mounting time, dusk,
pinning insects to cardboard squares,
labeling each catch with a familiar name:
swallowtail, monarch, black beetle, brown buggers,
black widow spiders, moths, crickets—not a
dragonfly among them—
waking up at midnight to insect symphonies:
wings flapping, bodies sobering
dusty feet scratching.

Aftermath

for Mary, my sister-in law

You left us in a hurry
 at forty
Canary yellow and confused
With a worn-out, useless liver
 which defied dialysis
We tried to understand
Your side of life
Daily drunks and nightly revelries
 briefly
Then argued about monuments
To erect in your memory, and
Exhibit to the world
What we forgot to tell you.

Swedish blue granite and
Polished black marble
We came to know headstones expertly
Perhaps better than we tried to know you
Still the unanswered phone calls
In the middle of nights past
 haunt us, hurt us
We hear your feeble voice
Electrically charged
Pleading for attention
Having so much to say, but
Refusing to let us know
 Your condition.

We should have honored you
Long before disputes over
Gravesites, wills, and life insurance—or
Your marriage of three months
A former husband, and
Two lovely daughters. But
Regrets are not enough to
Make your absence
More bearable
A jewel in the grass won't make
our neglect more justifiable.

Tomales Bay

Tomales Bay and Dillon's beach,
heaven to clam diggers, hell to children
brought together relatively
dysfunctional families out to best each other:
insults jumping body to body
like sand fleas hopping,
where seven-year-old fishermen
caught their first perch in
land-locked tide pools,
hands working effectively as net.

Oceanside bunkhouse
nights spent enclosed in
salt air sheets tucked
tightly, neatly…hospital corners
keep warm air circulating
just above damp bedspreads,
floor heater blasts
diminishing electricity,
knocking-out appliances with
each thermostatic matrix adjustment . . . .

Decades pass without much reflection.
Cousin John, today we brought you back,
tossed your ashes on the bay
white caps breaking, tides receding,
accepting your eternal charcoal reality,
peppering sand, evolving, becoming
top hats worn by fish and brine.

Without Wheels

Absinthe lips, cloudy mind preparing to flee,
milky perceptions push past clarity,
head hangs over a Moulin Rouge dreamscape,
hands grasp cards,
siblings laugh before I
etch a metamorphic moment
on their minds forever,
my chainsaw mumbling, fracturing
early morning tranquility without
intention,
seizure giving birth to a life its own,
moving on a journey as definite as the
Ford station wagon hospital haul,
family members wondering what I'd remember.

Images blurry, confounding:
vegetarians munching down on mandrake roots,
butterfly mandallas miscuing prosperity and good luck
Victoria's Secret sales girls wearing
shrink-wrap dresses and paper jewelry,
their credit card figures exquisitely braced
against tofu pocket books,
tossing cell phones like trinkets into wishing wells; all
stability's suspect, control as uncertain as
legs shimmying up greased lampposts;
life without wheels, untouchable—beyond
eight-fold paths or twelve-step programs—
alters meaning, builds temporal mountains
from breadcrumbs that sink like
Canada sucked into the belly of Florida.

Short breaths, muted screams
cry out for examination,
mouth rot dry as Denver's throat
seeks moisture, epileptic acceptance, lifelong endurance,
the dignity afforded silent winds championing
Don Quixote's ethics, chivalric code, or family values,
ideals forever laced like gauntlets, thrown at my feet
lasting quagmire of mucus, guilt, shame.
Sunshine's not on any astrological chart,
psychic reading, job description;
charity's no host to lives without wheels.

V.
Over the Shoulder

Directions

for Andrea

Gyrating opposite
Gravel-faced engineers and
Flabby, smooth-skinned suits.
Stayin' light, moving among
Stripped cars along side-streets of the El Camino
Only place that felt like home til' supplication from
Hilo, Saigon, San Blas, Cuzco, Nepal, B.C.
A smothering spiritual empire of
Sexy collarbones, waistlines, low backed tank-tops,
Tattooed wrists, and patchouli bodies.
Back then, BART pushed across landfill,
Burrowed under the San Francisco Bay, and just
Thinking of women felt like liposuction on gray matter.

Down the creek Andrea,
Raven-lipped mistress of shadows and delight—
Some say child abuse—would brush her
Taut breasts against my back,
I lay back into them
At eleven years old (onto them at fourteen)
Proposing to her in my mind,
Wondering what Monsignor Healy would say, would do
Given half a chance to tilt
His chalice in her direction.
She, with Kuma Sutra hands, Corinthian thighs, and
Chimney swept hair,
Left a young boy feeling like Tarzan, searching for the
Jewels of Opar, finding Glenda, the good witch—
Ah, where not any temptress or angel would do—
As intoxicating as fields of opiate poppies,
Cradling imagination, nurturing fascination,
Perplexing affection.

Patrician pretensions had no place, past or future
Amid Andrea's wilderness and natural inclinations, just as I
No longer slid between cars off the El Camino, and
Razors recovered an appearance of youth,
Andrea abandoned recent memory,
The nights embracing under Bo trees,
Fixing our immovable spot in the present, and the
Days of skinny dipping in water tanks and
Percolation ponds full of mosquito larva and algae—
Their growth never touched us nor we them
Yet they bit into an awareness
Cleft it clean with nowhere to progress.
Idyllic moments, defiant gestures--laying fireside friendly on
Scruffy, bearskin rugs, or stretching across streams
Like natural bridges
We wandered from windowpane romances and
Bath water ballrooms into
A world of terrycloth towels and other women.

Tracy and Ricardo

Tracy and Ricardo wore their VD
like social epaulettes everywhere they went—
penicillin queen and king—
high school sweethearts, never questioning who
breached their sacred relationship,
sharing more than calzoni with
another at Nick's Pizza.

Like cats staring out windows on rainy days
Tracy and Ricardo gazed at each other for
hours without judgment,
yet in consternation . . .
expecting secrets to unfold
like morning glories
day after day, year after year—
then close—
sealing, preserving all blossoms in
memory's sarcophagus.

Item aspirations drifted from
high times in pool halls to
low moments at the Geary Theater among
San Francisco's finest.
They milked popular culture,
sought out personal identity,
touched fragile, Braille dreams
like Tiffany glassware, cautionary, at a distance.

Troubleshooting mainframe computers at
General Electric,
Ricardo'd slap Tracy's saddlebags,
in front of fellow employees, and
she'd toss number 2 pencils at his gut.

Denying co-dependency,
shallowness led to indifference—fear—when
Tracy was diagnosed with breast cancer;
Ricardo refused to touch her
Red bandana handkerchief,
Kemo smooth head, or
Thin lizard hands.

Courtship on TWA

Filling the overhead luggage rack with a boom box
I thought she was Steffi Graf or Monica Seles
as she slipped her tennis racket under her seat
ready for any line shot that came her way.
She pulled out a magazine--THE magazine--on
teen love and 1500 guy secrets:
"Crazy Celebs,"
  wedding shockers,
        supermodels,
              beyond buff
       <u>Baywatch</u>
Behind the Trunks,
page after page,
the Stanford coed beamed at Kodak moments
imagining herself among the "beautiful people."

Glancing at the headline,
"What Guys Really Love and Hate,"
she rhythmically began tapping her foot,
snapping, clicking, and popping her gum crisply as if to
accentuate insights into the telling prose; then,
tossing aside her glossy paper courtship,
she stretched her neck like a doe
turned her attention to
 two five-year-old male toe heads
     across the isle
          who asked her to "pick a card--any card," but
never read the wonderland etched on her cheeks or
noticed a crying wilderness behind refinement in eyes.

Bird Legs

Raelyne called herself *Bird Legs*
although no one knew why; with a
statuesque figure inviting classic comparisons, her
desert spring effervescence
suggested only perfection, a beauty—
tall, elegant, assured, enchanting,
flung among bodies incarcerated in
middle school madness. She
stretched her thighs
unfolded slender arms, like
delicate fairie wings fluttering, wind catching,
curling about worshipers, creating
snow angel sheets,
teaching French, her skilled snake tongue darting,
engendering love's finer moments,
transitory answers, then immobility,
concluding in salamander sadness; with
pillbox possibilities, Raelyne
baptized us all with genuine tears,
borrowed smiles, and fossilized laughter.

In a world of box top dividends, we
redeemed fleeting passion
tried to make it enduring, while
Bird Legs made the most of our
elastic lives, wrapped her
limbs around raging pomp and circumstance,
our inexperience, as if
born to make a difference beyond
locker room celebrity,
rock concert courtships, and
trailer park trysts.

Sylvia and I

Sylvia and I sat in opposite corners,
she, a person allowed visitations
only with a chaperon
her aunt
needle eyed harpy
as ancient as
Babylonian gardens,
forgiving as any vigilante,
knitted Costa Rican quilts as we spoke,
weighing our words with the
measured precision of a medieval apothecary
just waiting for glances or vocabulary to censure.

The living room rug between us got old
while Sylvia's passions blossomed into
Catholic girl intensity and earthy devotion;
I, a lone figure of guilt, contemplated opportunity,
in fascination and terror, watched
traditional cultural values tossed aside like old clothes, as
Sylvia celebrated assimilation among San José's populace,
subdued by the same magic as Miranda's
brave new world wonders.

After buying me *Surrealistic Pillow,*
the metaphor and core of our romance,
she'd sneak out nights wearing
a long coat and boots,
pelt my bedroom window with pea gravel,
signaling a successful household break; primed to
meet in wooden tract home frames, we'd
revel in the shadows, rolling amid sawdust,
scraping against metal socket slugs,
staring at stars through unshingled roofs,
walking home in different directions,
one categorizing details for this week's confession,
the other leaving Rome even farther behind.

Earth 'n' Shadow

I

Resourceful stylist,
Cynthia wore cut-off denim overalls
neither underwear nor blouse
beneath suspendered farm girl shoulders
left upper arm encircled, a Celtic knot tattoo, a
brass serpent coiled around flesh of the right, her
almond shaped small pox vaccination hidden
beneath folds in the cold metal scales.

Cynthia the earth,
her mother the moon, showcased
henna hands, Mendhi painting
lines leading to life-affirming forces
near eastern customs and
Cynthia's Wiccan ways, balancing rural and city
attuning herself to nature's rhythms,
wisdom's rhymes;
she, a spirited tarot card waiting to be read,
seduced the light and dark side around her,
decorating her poetry like the *Book of Kells*,
ever the priestess, who
like an illustrated manuscript
read her verse with flair and color
anytime summoned for jury duty.

II

Five year Heather,
terra firma's child,
loved her mother wholly,
despised all lovers, eternally,
melted into hallway shadows,
floor furnace foxholes and
dustball barricades. She'd
lean like wind blown grass against winter clothes in
Cynthia's closet, absorbing the soil scent of
her mother's pregnant cotton fabric
hyperventilating, fixating upon a
silhouette undulating, singular,
as Cynthia and I became one.

Heather through dark crevices crept
as silence embraced us all and
rolling waterbed waves abated; then
began serious Siren audibles,
like canyon echoes, loud and sharp mellowing to
shaky, and faint, Heather summoned her
earth mother's madness, demanding maternal comfort,
receiving curt orders for quiet from she at my side.
Like a self conscious sailor in Steubenville,
feeling like a dusty coal barge on the Ohio river,
filthy and offensive, I rose to
quit the epidermal tryst when
Heather's metamorphic shadow struck, awakening
my nightmare's soul, the altered state of the other within. So
fled mother and child from my awareness; my retreat, as slow
as caravan wheels turning in mud,
sinking into subdued light, moon iridescence,
leaving them both attentive to each other again.

The Entertainer

For Scott, my brother

Fishing on backs of horseshoe crabs
Spiked spines cracking between toes, waving to
Gnat-sized cliff figures; weeping as ocean perch
Gave live birth in a bucket.

Brew some coffee, light a smoke
Praise all your cats, groom Chester, your horse;
Remembrance, like prayers, provide
Ritual observance, exorcizing emptiness. Scott
Like the forceful, flowing creek through Brookdale Lodge
Ignited imagination, encouraged humor, created melancholy.

Blood red walls
Marilyn Monroe shrine offset with
Batman memorabilia and small wooden bowls
Showcase a theatrical history from
Christ in *Godspell* to messenger in *1776*; yet
Following an operation and malpractice suit
Like a continual solar eclipse, your
Theatrical bright star fell into
A hazy, blackened horizon--misty vista where
Skylights devour shadows, the sun's
Warm rays reflected.

We miss you Scott, Broadway's best
The Bard's Jacques; who
Knew the seven ages of man
Taking cues from nobody,
Moving from soap opera vespers to big budget film cameos,
Exiting center stage, evolving into a celebrity—
A piano bar favorite—then a voice sought for
Christenings, birthdays, weddings, funerals; the
Ode to Joy you sang to me being no exception.

A September song sings nothing but blue notes,
Drawing siblings to San Lorenzo River's beach—place
Down a hill getting harder to ascend, just
As boardwalk nights with Rock 'n Roll has-beens
Became difficult to endure.
Still we reveled with the Spoonful, one last autumn night, got
Temporary tattoos to make mother proud
You wore yours to a hospital, then a
Place facing west where you'd never have to rise.

The Actress

Pink blouse,
cuffs upturned,
draw immediate attention to her wrists—
    the beauties
weighted down with woven bars of gold,
    delicate pieces of art and someone else's passion and pain;
the actress leisurely thumbs through her lines,
catching every ray of light she can
    on her magnificent bracelets;
with carefully sculptured kite-string fingers
which meet at the ridges like
boxed-in canyons on her palms,
she reads along highlighted passages in a whisper;
but the feverish pitch of her sustained intensity
calls attention to the swelling plateaus of veins
which rise like teal piano wires
on the top of her hands.

American Airlines lands on time in San Jose, but
while pedestrian hands move towards luggage racks,
the actress sits quietly—rests composed,
    slips on the shoes she took off in Nashville, and
        waits for the mad rush for the door to subside,
then rises with dignity, grace, and assurance,
twists the precious metal ingots around her wrists three times,
    and walks off the plane to board her connecting flight
        to Burbank.

ABOUT THE AUTHOR

Over the last 30 years, Sterling Warner has taught a wide variety of Composition, Literature, Creative Writing, and Rhetoric courses at two and four year colleges and universities. The author of fiction, non-fiction, and poetry, Warner's works include: *THRESHOLDS (© 1997), PROJECTIONS: BRIEF READINGS ON AMERICAN CULTURE* (2nd edition © 2003), *WORLD LITERATURE AND INTRODUCTION TO THEATRE (5th* edition © 2008), and *VISIONS ACROSS THE AMERICAS (8th edition* © *2013).* His poems have appeared in several literary magazines and journals, including *IN THE GROVE, THE CHAFFEY REVIEW, LEAF BY LEAF, THE MONTEREY REVIEW, INSIDE ENGLISH, THE MESSENGER, FACULTY MATTERS, THE ATHERTON REVIEW,* and *METAMORPHSES.* Additionally, Warner also published three collections of poetry: *WITHOUT WHEELS* (In the Grove Press © 2005), *SHADOWCAT: POEMS*, and *EDGES: POEMS* (Maple Press © 2012)—as well as *MEMENTO MORI: A CHAPBOOK* (Maple Press ©2010). A Jim Herndon Award recipient (2013) as well as a Hayward Award winner (2000), Warner was named the Atherton Poet Laureate in 2014. Currently, Warner teaches in the English Department at Evergreen Valley College, where he has served as the Creative Writing Program Director, The Evergreen Valley College Author's Series Organizer, the *LEAF BY LEAF* literary magazine Chief Editor, and the *Evergreen Valley College Annual Spring Poetry Festival Coordinator.*